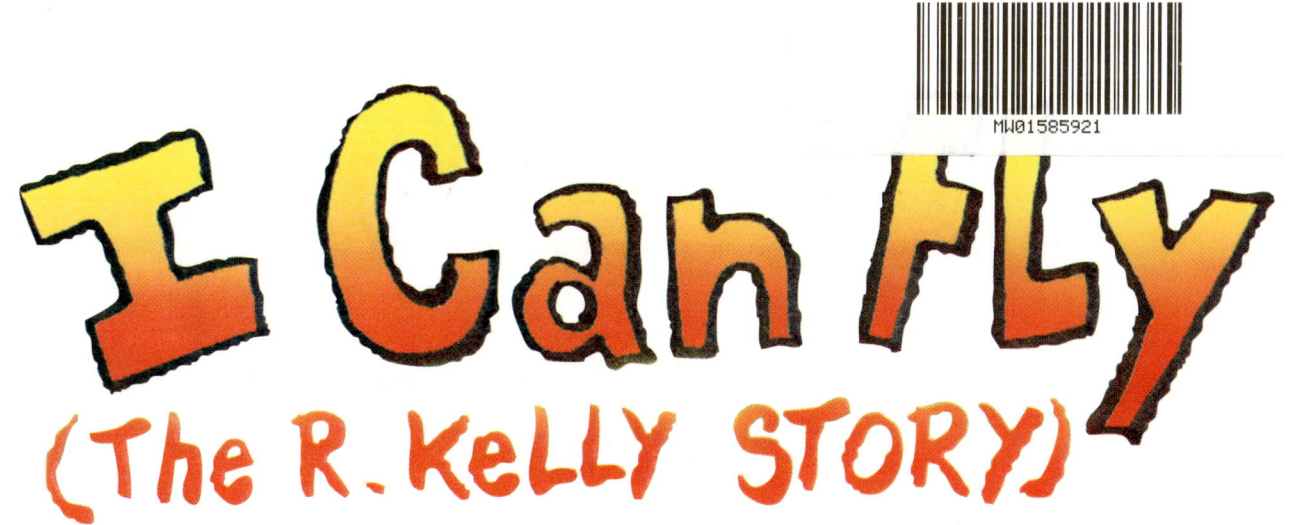

I Can Fly
(The R. Kelly Story)

For
Joanne
and
young dreamers around the world.

WRITTEN BY: KIM DULANEY
ILLUSTRATED BY: RONALD DEANE

Copyright©
1998 Kim Dulaney
All Rights Reserved
Printed in the USA

No part of this publication may be reproduced, stored in a retrieval system, or transmitted in any form or by any means, electronic, mechanical, photocopying, recording or otherwise, without the prior consent of the publisher.

Published By:
Unique Expressions
A Division of Finders Keepers, Inc.
P.O. Box 11869
Chicago, Illinois 60611
e-mail: readme4000@aol.com
1-888-README4

Printed By

317-329-9974
Fax 317-216-7148
6212 La Pas Trail
Indianapolis, IN 46268

ISBN 1-891636-03-0

In elementary school, he was the guy,
who said he believed, that he could fly.
Everyone laughed at him
and thought he was crazy.
They said he was confused,
or maybe just lazy.

He was a different kind of kid:
He would sing songs into his mic
which was actually a broom,
as he'd imagine there were a million people
crowded in the room.

His mother was so proud of him
she'd attend every show,
and when the show was over,
they'd realize they were still...in the ghetto.
Still, he believed he could fly!

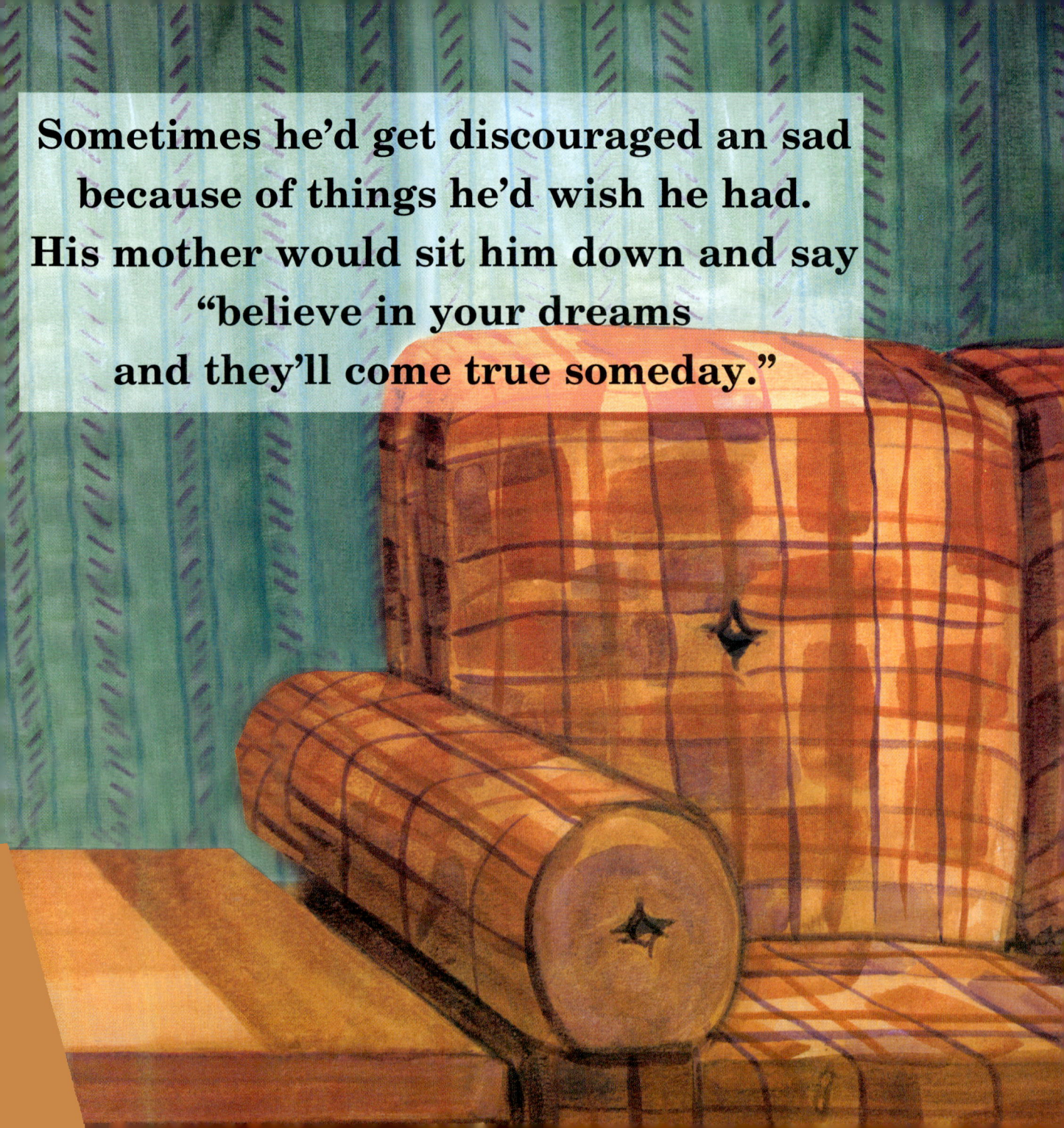

Sometimes he'd get discouraged an sad because of things he'd wish he had. His mother would sit him down and say "believe in your dreams and they'll come true someday."

**Now he has <u>some</u> money
and he's recorded lots of songs.
But everyday, believe it or not,
he still dreams all day long.**

**Before he knew he'd work with Batman,
he painted the emblem in his pool.
Then, to keep the fun flowing
he decided more cartoon characters
would be cool.**

Since basketball is his favorite sport, he painted an audience of characters around his basketball court.

Now listen closely
and pay attention to what you just read.
The point is...
When he put those pictures in his house,
they were just dreams in his head.

Then one day to his surprise,
they asked him to sing songs for movies
starring these guys!

It was amazing to see,
the way that his dreams
had prepared him, for these great things.

Sometimes when he's all alone late at night, he has to think to himself...
"Mama was right!"
If you can see it, you can be it.
Just as long as *you* believe it!

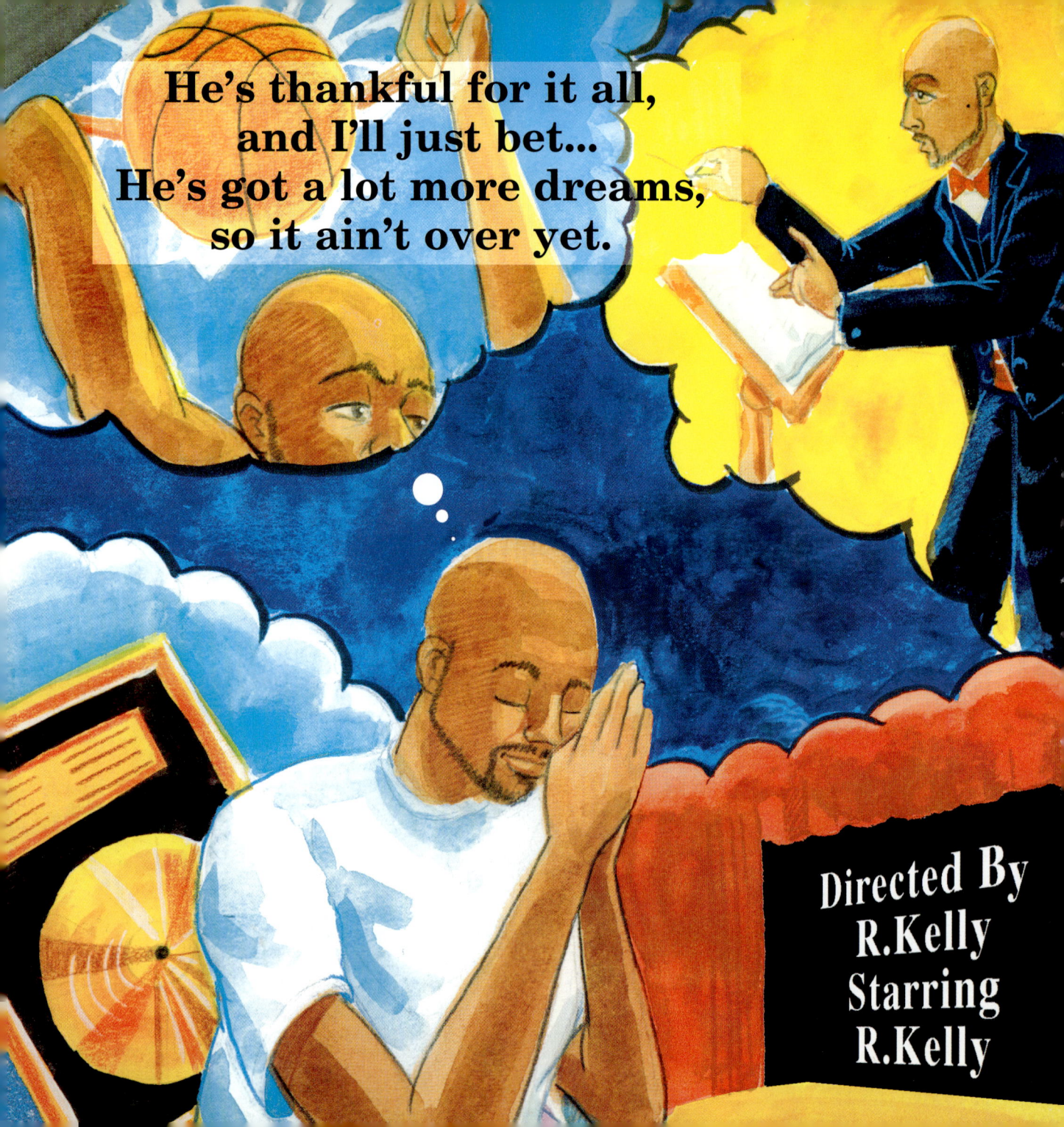

The moral of this story is?

A: You can be anything you want

B: Follow your dreams

C: Believe in yourself

D: God is good

E: All of the above